Women lawyers from around the world share their hopes for the future

IN HER WORDS

D'APRÈS ELLE 用她自己的话 EZISHOLO YENA

Edited by
D. DENIS-SMITH AND A. VAN DE CASTEELE
with
NEXT 100 YEARS

SCALA

INTRODUCTION

Smile! Hold still! And #FaceTheFuture! And then the whole world came to a standstill.

On March 5th and 6th 2020 many of our colleagues around the world gathered in a single room for the same purpose: to have their portrait taken as part of the Next 100 Years campaign to create a visual image of the world's legal profession in 2020.

Unaware of what lay ahead as COVID-19 was beginning to spread globally, there was a strong sense of camaraderie during those two photography days. Across 23 locations around the world from Sydney to Glasgow to Mexico City, women, men, and sometimes even their children, came together to provide a collective and, as it turned out, historic snapshot of the legal profession in over 1,000 portraits.

On those two days, the rise and rise of women in the legal profession seemed certain. The portrait emerging was one of diversity and optimism. We were all feeling that in the future the legal profession would be more inclusive, that women would break through to lead and build on the legacy of the pioneers before them. But as 2020 unfolded, it started to provide a worrying picture of how much of the progress made by women in the previous century could be reversed by a global shock.

This is purposefully a collection of portraits and subsequent reflections by ordinary women lawyers reflecting on their hopes for the future as the pandemic forced them to stop and stand still for longer than any of us could have envisaged on those special days in March 2020. We are delighted to create this physical memento of 2020, so that future generations may understand the legal world as it was for us.

Dana Denis-Smith

AFRICA

The progress of women in law across Africa has been uneven and sometimes faltering, but always studded with shining stars. In 1908, Blanche Azoulay became the first woman lawyer in Algeria, and her achievement was recorded with fanfare in the Paris press. In 1966, Princess Elizabeth of Toro, also a highly successful fashion model, became the first woman lawyer in Uganda. A year earlier, she had become the first East African woman called to the Bar of England and Wales. 2007 saw Georgina Wood become the first woman Chief Justice of Ghana. In what is hopefully the beginning of a move from isolated 'firsts' to a new wave of female representation, Somalia saw the country's first women public prosecutors hired in 2015 – six at once.

Justice Georgina Wood, former Chief Justice of Ghana

The last few decades have witnessed remarkable strides in equality and diversity of women in law in Ghana, and indeed other countries on the African continent. In academia, on the Bench and in both corporate and private legal practice, women have attained heights hitherto regarded as the preserve of their male counterparts. May the successes achieved so far in this advocacy propel many more aspirations and realisations of equality and diversity in the ever-growing legal profession of our world.

Lerato Molefi
Cape Town

I am a young woman in the law: my career has just begun, and
while the barriers to entry that have always existed for women are
still there, they are beginning to subside. The law is transforming
across all spheres, be it racial, cultural or even intellectual. I hope
that the barriers to entry will one day cease to exist as the law stands
for equality, freedom and transformation. This is my hope for the
future of this profession: that we identify the purpose of the law and
live it truthfully and with conviction.

Rita Namakiika Nangono
Kampala

The pandemic exacerbated the struggles of many women in law. In my case, the closure of schools meant that I was both mother and teacher to my four children. Empty courts and a struggling economy mean that I have lost ground in my career. However, we have seen developments such as the emergence of legal tech firms, and the economic downturn has created demand for legal services. The pandemic has strengthened my resolve to be creative and innovative, so there is hope. I am determined to rise from the ashes like the phoenix!

Anek Trinity Daisy
Kampala

The pandemic presented an opportunity for me to relax my busy schedule. However, remote working presented its own challenges, like how to juggle work with house chores – predominantly a female role in Uganda. Fortunately, technology enabled me to balance work with most of my other commitments. My hopes for the future are that we can embrace technology in the legal field, especially in developing countries, and encourage remote and flexible working. This will improve the mental health of many employees and allow them to thrive in their career and personal life.

7

THE AMERICAS

North and South America have a long tradition of pioneering legal women, seeing some of the first women lawyers in the world. In the USA, Arabella A. Mansfield became the country's first woman lawyer in 1869, followed soon after by the first African American woman lawyer, Charlotte E. Ray in 1872. The first woman lawyer qualified in Peru in 1892 and in Mexico in 1898. More recently, the Americas have continued this tradition by producing internationally significant women leaders in the law, such as Ruth Bader Ginsburg from the USA and Argentina's Silvia Fernández de Gurmendi, who in 2015 was elected the first woman president of the International Criminal Court.

The Right Hon. Beverley McLachlin PC CC CStJ, former Chief Justice of Canada

I certainly didn't grow up thinking I'd be a lawyer. But I did think that I wanted to do something different and to be independent. I saw people like my mother who were the beneficiaries of what they called first-wave feminism, which was to get the legal rights, get the right to vote and everything would be fine. And things weren't fine, so I thought something needed to change... So, I went down to my little town, which is in the ranching district of Southern Alberta, and wrote to the Dean and said, 'Will you give me some information on studying law?', and he wrote back and said, 'You're admitted.'

Jenny Ferrón
Mexico City

I'm hoping sorority is our new normal as working women. Also, I hope women around the world have the support and tools they need to take charge of the direction of their career; have access to a social and financial ecosystem that helps them thrive without carrying unnecessary or gender-imposed burdens that may limit their growth or force them to make decisions they wouldn't otherwise make.

Ana Paula Tellería Ramírez
Mexico City

I am the lucky mother of two babies. Being a partner in one of the top law firms in Mexico and a mother is one of the most extreme balancing acts I could ever have imagined, especially in a country which still has a long way to go regarding education on female equality. Being confined, taking care of my kids and working from home has been challenging to the extreme, exhausting. The support of my spouse and his acknowledgement that taking care of our kids and doing chores is both our responsibility, equally, really shows that it is the support of men, of them stepping up, which allows for the breach that exists between us professionally to grow less wide.

Ivette Montero
Mexico City

Being a woman in the legal profession has been an amazing experience. I finished law school in 1998. Since then, I have had the opportunity to work as an in-house lawyer. It all became rather challenging when I had children. In 2015, I switched from doing corporate work to the social arena. That year I founded a non-profit organisation, providing services and support to non-profit organisations and vulnerable groups.

Running and leading a pro bono organisation in Mexico during any contingency is quite a challenge. Society in general and vulnerable groups in particular need guidance and legal support to have access to justice. This pandemic has been no exception and, so far, it has been the most challenging contingency ever faced.

Over the last few months, adapting to my children's new school rules and different family dynamics and, at the same time, being focused on a demanding workload to achieve goals have all been tough tasks. The role played by women in the profession has been critical. Many pro bono woman lawyers work even harder taking into consideration the work overload in the office and at home. However, it has been highly motivating to witness the coordinated will of the united Mexican legal community to support those most in need. The pandemic has also opened a broad window of opportunity to innovate and to demonstrate that things may be done differently, and the same or even better results may be obtained. This strongly signals the existence of a humane, empathic and united legal community that is willing to fight for a fairer society, one that we all yearn for and need.

Daniela Cuéllar Müller
Mexico City

I would summarise it in three ways: i) home working; ii) female networks; iii) female leadership.

First, I can attest to how the pandemic has sped up the understanding of, and acceptance for working from home. Just a few months ago, a stigma prevailed at the institutional level; however, an ever-growing body of evidence regarding its benefits has become too strong to be ignored.

Second, I have also experienced that women in crisis are extremely empathetic and waste no time creating aid networks beyond their families – not to mention women in the medical-care frontline. It has made me realise something I had thought intuitively: women can address problems combining clear-headedness with empathy and humility.

Such a combination – in authority or power – leads me to the third point: female leaders as role models. As a matter of fact, pandemic responses led by women have been consistently successful. Therefore it will be essential to get to know those leaders' stories and voices.

Being a lawyer with experience in the banking and public sector has shown me that it is essential to raise our voice helping and supporting more female engagement. The task is far from over, but the potential benefits are indeed wide.

Karla Patricia Nieto Contreras
Mexico City

No doubt no one expected an event of this magnitude with the different consequences that it has triggered. We have seen the impact economically, socially, politically, culturally and in other aspects such as the increase in domestic violence, the new dynamics in families, the subsistence of older adults, unemployment, and people who have had to go out and undertake different tasks.

Likewise, abruptly and due to the responsibility and response of companies to this COVID-19 pandemic, we have had to work from home, a practice that in my country was not customary, but to which collaborators have responded favourably, maintaining or increasing productivity. As a result of this situation, families have also had to adapt, with students taking classes via the web (raising the problem of insufficient computer equipment for family members and reduced space in the home). Women have had to play the role of active professionals, take online courses, help children take classes via the web, doing homework with them, and also attend to food and various household and recreational tasks.

On the other hand, technological advances have been an important factor, enabling us to carry out new activities electronically. In Mexico, on the subject of litigation, some trials and hearings have been started electronically, but this has only been authorised in a few cities and only for certain types of procedure and trial, affecting the trial lawyers, clients and their situations, until the activities are re-established.

Government initiatives have enabled progress in the private sector in the drawing up of contracts and other documents electronically, ensuring that this can be done securely and so avoiding possible opposition to litigation where the absence of a signature renders the documents invalid.

Looking to positive developments in the legal profession, we must keep an open mind so that these new challenges bring about change. It would be a great advance if procedures could be carried out online, helping to save the time lost in travelling to the different places where administrative and judicial institutions are located, or to other cities where our work takes us. Further, if we can consult the entire online file without having to go to these institutions in person, it would help qualified lawyers to serve clients, rather than the many people who call themselves lawyers and are not: this would protect clients and professionals alike.

The above would be a great step in the profession, providing great value by contributing to practicality, agility and minimal use of paper, which would also help sustainability on the planet, leaving the world a better place for the next generations.

Regina Yarto
Mexico City

As I am at the beginning of my career, this was my first experience of balancing my work and doing 'what is expected of you as a woman' in household chores. The one thing I must express is my respect to all of those women who run a household and work in an area as demanding as law can be.

I hope that this situation (COVID), which is holding us back in so many aspects of life, will help us to take many steps forward in order to achieve equality and to realise how important cooperation between men and women is in order to empower ourselves and be better in everything we do.

Gender empowerment doesn't mean discrimination, it only means equality.

ASIA PACIFIC

The story of women in law in Asia is marked from the beginning by remarkable and determined figures. Natividad Almeda-López became the first practising woman lawyer in the Philippines in 1914. A vocal feminist, she gave an impassioned speech arguing for women's rights before the country's legislature. China's Tcheng Yu-hsiu became the country's first woman lawyer in 1926 and, later, its first woman judge, and sat in Shanghai. Jenny Lau Buong Be made history in not one but two countries: as Malaysia's first woman magistrate and Singapore's first woman judge. Today, the progress of women in law varies greatly and reflects the continent's diversity of cultures, languages and levels of legal sector development.

Meanwhile, New Zealand and Australia both saw women gain access to the legal profession while part of the British Empire but before their counterparts in the UK. In 1897 New Zealand's Ethel Benjamin was admitted as a solicitor and a barrister, soon becoming the first woman to appear as counsel before court in the British Empire. In Australia, a campaign by Flos Greig, who would go on to become Australia's first woman lawyer, led to the Parliament of Victoria passing the Women's Disabilities Removal Act 1903 to permit women to practise. Since then, Australia has seen its first woman Chief Justice (Susan Kiefel) and so has New Zealand (Dame Sian Elias). Though the representation of women in the profession remains patchy across the rest of the region, recent victories have included Samoa's Brenda Heather-Latu being appointed the first woman Attorney General in the country (and region) in 1997 and Papua New Guinea's Nerrie Eliakim becoming its first woman Chief Magistrate in 2013.

The Hon. Chief Justice Susan Kiefel AC, Chief Justice of Australia

When I was called to the Bar in 1975 women lawyers faced many challenges. Much has been achieved. Women from diverse backgrounds are to be found in every aspect of the practice of law and legal education and in senior positions. This is evident from the stories in the Asia Pacific section. Their voices and their claims to true equality of opportunity will be heard.

Sam Phey
Singapore

I am lucky to have entered the profession alongside a trainee intake comprising similar proportions of women and men, with a firm committed to having at least 40% female partners by 2030. Since my photo was taken as part of the 'Face the Future' campaign, the pandemic has brought upon women, in the law and in so many other industries, an unprecedented merger of the workplace and the home. For the foreseeable future, lawyers are set to continue working from home, with many female lawyers now simultaneously wearing two hats, managing both their professional and home desks.

There is a saying that goes, 'Women hold up half the sky,' that women are equally capable of performing in a professional environment. Over the years, we've witnessed an increasing trend of women in law, which we should continue to support and celebrate. We forget that men hold up the other half of the sky – I hope for a world where we might come to regard ourselves as holding indistinguishable halves to a collective whole, and together we hold up the entire sky. I hope that we will come to share and work at both desks.

The Honourable Margaret Beazley AC QC
Sydney

My experience as a woman in the law from the mid-1970s ran
the gamut of extreme discrimination to significant support. The
discriminatory aspects included exclusion from many sets of
chambers, exclusion from various areas of work, withdrawal of
briefs if a partner realised a woman had been briefed, and sexual
harassment.

These experiences taught me two major lessons: to keep going,
with humour where possible; and to pick the time and issues on
which to speak up. This was a profession I loved, and I intended to
stay in it and to succeed. Overall, the judges were supportive and
gradually there was a shift in the culture at the Bar, although not
nearly enough, as many of these problems persist. I saw that money
was power. Equal pay is thus essential to redress power imbalances
and to ensure equality. Women excel in the profession and the law
must have diverse voices.

On 2 May 2019, I left the law to take up my appointment as the
39th Governor of New South Wales. In this role, I seek to put all
my experiences to use, positive or otherwise, in the service of the
people of New South Wales.

Fiona Le
Sydney

I was working as a Legal Administration Officer at the Office of the Fair Work Ombudsman. My experience is that there are more women in the law working in the public sector. In fact, the current and previous Fair Work Ombudsmen were both women!

So much has changed over the last few months. Due to the impact of coronavirus on workplaces, there has been a number of changes to workplace laws. For example, a new entitlement to paid 'pandemic leave' for residential aged-care employees (of whom a large proportion are women).

My hope for the future of the profession is for more Asian Australian diversity in leadership to reflect the Australian community. I hope to see more Asian Australian partners in law firms and hopefully the first Asian Australian judge on the High Court of Australia.

Natalie Silver
Sydney

As a legal academic and a mother, the past few months have been difficult. The onset of the pandemic required significant personal and professional adjustments. Balancing work commitments with online schooling for three children was particularly challenging. University teaching moved online, providing significant pedagogical challenges as many students struggled under imperfect learning conditions. Promising research collaborations and conferences overseas were postponed. On a societal level, the inequities that exist in Australia and throughout the world have been illuminated during the pandemic. It is my hope that the legal profession, through a diverse range of careers and pro bono roles, will continue to use the law to address the rights of those suffering from disadvantage and to promote a more just society.

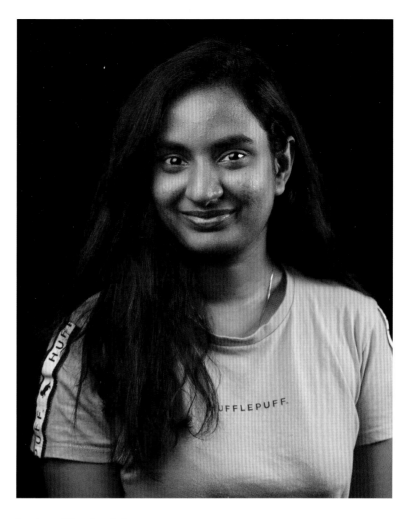

Luckme Vimalarajah
Sydney

Working and studying from home was exciting at the very start
of the pandemic. Since I live far away from the city, I saved a lot
of time travelling and was able to spend more time for myself and
with my family, but as time passed I missed seeing my colleagues
and catching up with them for lunch. In the future I hope for more
flexible and adaptable workplaces.

Kimberlee Weatherall
Sydney

The legal and academic professions have relationships and justice at their heart. Never in my life have these been so important – or faced such trials. Relationships – local and global – are challenging without the ability to be physically together. I found personally that as a teacher, the sudden shift to screen-mediated classes with everyone in their very different homes meant we all had to work that much harder to communicate, to debate and to learn. Law students rose to the occasion, but everyone struggled. And because the pandemic was affecting us all in different ways, fairness and justice – in the classroom and in society – have been harder to guarantee. The cracks have been showing and many of the burdens have fallen on women. My hope? That we take the opportunity to build back better: better universities and a more just society. I'm worried – there are plenty who would, given the chance, take advantage of this crisis to wind back civil liberties, extend surveillance and other controls. So I can't think of a more critical time for all of us to be paying attention to how the law can better protect the most vulnerable and protect fundamental rights and democratic values.

EUROPE

The story of Europe's first woman lawyer begins in Italy...
or does it? In 1883, Lidia Poët became the first woman
in Italy inscribed on the roll of advocates. However, a
subsequent court case found that her inscription was
illegal, leading to uproar and a movement to allow women
to practise law in the country. Meanwhile in France, the turn
of the century saw Olga Petit and Jeanne Chauvin become
the first female lawyers in France in 1900, with Jeanne
being the first to plead a case before a French court. Turkey
is notable for appointing the first female supreme court
judge in the world, Melahat Ruaca in 1945.

The 1980s and 1990s saw the number of women studying
law grow dramatically, leading to increased representation
among lawyers in many European countries. To this day,
however, higher-ranking judicial positions are largely
dominated by men, the gender pay gap remains and
countries such as France have seen the 'feminisation'
of the law result in declining prestige.

Laura Kövesi, European Chief Prosecutor

'The prosecutor's office is not for women' was
the first thing I heard when I started as a
prosecutor 25 years ago. Throughout my entire
career, I have had to work harder than my male
colleagues to prove that I could do the job. I
encountered many obstacles but never gave up.
For me, to be a woman in law means to gain
the trust of the people and, more importantly, to
succeed in keeping it. This is only possible by
working professionally and by respecting the law
at all times. The most important thing is to not
be alone, and to work with people who believe in
the same goal.

Rhian Ravenscroft
Amsterdam

I love my job and career, but working in the city with a corporate law background, I have at times found the lack of change and innovation in the way the legal profession operates incredibly frustrating. The general lack of flexibility and a sceptical view of remote working is, in my eyes, damaging and limits the careers of those with other demands outside of work (whether that be a family, care responsibilities, pro bono work or other passions) or of those who don't fit the conventional mould of what a lawyer is expected to be. Whilst I've found any limitations imposed on me were mitigated by a move in-house to a more forward-thinking company, my hope is that we, as lawyers, take the positive from this crisis and together build a better, more flexible approach to working which adapts to the individual. We should embrace the change that was brought by the pandemic, continue to work efficiently without needing total presenteeism in an office at all hours of the day (and night) and continue to treat our colleagues and our profession with empathy and understanding. I believe this will retain talent, help support diversity and encourage those less traditionally represented at the top of our profession.

Laurence Azoux Bacrie
Paris

'The quality of a society is measured by the way it treats its women.' This was the verdict of the UNESCO Bioethics Committee in 2002, which was concerned with the impact of progress in life sciences on the condition of women. COVID-19 has thrown into sharp relief the link between isolation at home and violence against women. The victims of this violence are a central concern of the rights of mankind and universal human rights. Domestic confinement has revealed the dysfunctional state of sexual inequality, with regard to violence but also in the extent to which women have had to take on remote working alongside household chores and looking after their husband and children. The aim of the State Department for Equality between Men and Women is to strengthen the legal protection offered to women, and one of its most alarming discoveries is a significant increase in domestic violence – police intervention in such cases has risen by 44% compared to 2019. Paradoxically, while the reporting of these incidents has increased, fewer cases have resulted in legal action.

One of the highest priorities for the Ministry for Europe and Foreign Affairs this government term is the promotion of gender equality and the fight against discrimination. France has pushed for the Istanbul Convention to be ratified internationally. As the guardians of liberty lawyers must ensure that the law is adapted to respond effectively.

Caroline Violas
Paris

I chose this career in order to help humanity. What I hope, therefore, is that we can get back to speaking to one another. Without the spoken word there is no humanity.

Jade Paya
Paris

I was at law school when the pandemic began. Since then I have had to work remotely, which has disrupted human relations entirely. Opportunities to meet future colleagues have been extremely limited. It is even more complicated to find your feet as a woman, a situation exacerbated by the pandemic which has tended to isolate people.

I hope, once the pandemic is over, that I will be able to meet legal professionals, speak with them and learn from them – in short, to be able to carry out my future profession freely.

Hélène Lecat
Paris

The judiciary, already weakened over the course of many years, is now in a similar state of disarray as society itself, and seems to have made the carrying out of justice even harder.

After several months spent fighting a particularly unjust and injurious retirement reform, the pandemic was upon us – what, then, is the future of our profession, the last bulwark of fundamental freedoms?

The current health crisis appears to be confirming and accentuating the fragility of our democratic institutions, since now more than ever essential human relations are missing from an increasingly dehumanised justice system (remote working, legal proceedings without a hearing, etc.). The law must strive to establish and maintain contact between people.

I hope that in the near future we will be able to find a happy medium between managing the health crisis and safeguarding our democracy. A society stripped of human contact makes no sense. I know that our profession will keep an even closer eye on the rights of defendants, while fighting as hard as possible to create a world united, at last, in its care for the health and ecological environment of all communities.

Johanna Ropars
Paris

Being a woman and a lawyer is an everyday struggle to prove that I deserve the position I occupy and that I belong to this profession as much as anyone else. The pandemic we are facing today is changing the way we all work. Personally, it makes me think that we're all human beings and our gender, our skin colour and so on are irrelevant. We all need to reinvent ourselves and keep being positive for the future.

Corinne Lasnier Berose
Paris

This photograph was taken in March 2020 (the year of my 50th birthday) as part of the 'Face the Future' project bringing together women working in the law, a few days before Paris was hit by the health crisis caused by the COVID-19 pandemic and the authorities imposed lockdown. We were all gathered together that day, but none of us knew what extraordinary times we were about to experience. Since then, the pandemic has had a huge, unprecedented impact on our lives, our expectations and the way in which we carry out our professional activities.

Our legal practice (a small outfit comprising three women – two lawyers and an assistant) was restricted by the closing of the courthouses, but fortunately home working and access to courts online have allowed us to maintain contact with our clients, proceed with cases and attend to any urgent business remotely.

We have had to adapt in record time, reconciling our professional, personal and family lives while confined to our homes. This 'slowing down' period has provided an opportunity to reflect and re-evaluate, as we must be conscious of our priorities when considering the choices we make, in particular the health of all those around us, and more generally the need for justice, solidarity and due care in our relationship with our environment.

On the face of it, it is difficult to step back and analyse the impact the health crisis has had on the legal profession, since the straitened economic situation is set to last for months or longer – for now, we must survive the crisis.

Given the constant need to implement successive reforms and new modes of practice, to learn and adapt, lawyers today are unrecognisable from their counterparts in 2000. The law is in a perpetual state of adaptation to meet the needs of a changing society, and the legal profession has undergone unprecedented transformation. The current crisis demands that we reinvent ourselves once again and devise solutions that we hope will be positive.

Stéphanie Ginestal
Paris

The current pandemic, which hit us nearly six months ago as I write this, struck my profession with full force.

My work has been heavily impacted by the health crisis. Throughout the lockdown courts have been closed and only extremely urgent cases have been pursued. Since I cannot meet clients in person, new work has been thin on the ground.

Nevertheless, I have made efforts to maintain contact with my clients and respond to them as well as I can. This has been made possible by technology, and email, phone and video-conferencing have been very useful during the lockdown.

Face-to-face meetings and court hearings have partially returned, but these new tools are still very helpful in my day-to-day work as I have to restrict meetings in person.

The worry never goes away, but we have to face up to this cruel virus that could strike any one of us… The world has changed but more than ever my defence is the same – I owe it to myself to be by my clients' side, to be there for them and defend them to the best of my ability.

Anouschka Zagorski
Vienna

When I started private practice in 1993, women had to work twice as hard as men to get ahead. They would only be able to combine a full-time legal career with having children if they were able to afford 24/7 childcare.

Being a mother whilst pursuing a career path was barely accepted. This has changed over the last decades, and more so over the lockdown period in the spring of 2020. With everyone being at home, it became normal to hold audio or video meetings with children in the background. People started to relate to one another and realise that a professional is also a human being.

My hope for the future is that the (legal) business world continues to be increasingly mindful, inclusive and accepting of different ways practitioners want to combine their work and their home life.

Dr Ursula Kriebaum
Vienna

Working from home, online teaching, cancelled conferences, online presentations… My hopes are that we can cope with the pandemic on a global level and can again meet in person – we can certainly use the experience we have gained during this difficult period and hopefully can combine it with all the possibilities we have missed during the pandemic.

Dajana Bjelovuk
Vienna

A week after the picture was taken, a global pandemic changed all
our lives.

My perception of what work is and where it is done from
changed within a day, due to the rapid shift to working remotely.
As a legal assistant to a group of national and international lawyers,
I suddenly faced a completely different working environment, not
being used to working from home. I did adapt quickly to the new
situation, but at the same time I missed my team. We organised
short daily meetings in order to keep up the team spirit. During
those unprecedented times, I believe it was more important than
ever to communicate honestly and openly.

Now after a storm of changes, I am back in the office again. I feel
like the team spirit has become even stronger and that we have a
higher social awareness, also organising lunch breaks and after-work
dinners together. Additionally, now I enjoy the possibility of working
flexibility as the team knows that I can provide them with precise
legal and administrative support even when I work remotely.

UNITED
KINGDOM

Before 1919, women were legally barred from entering a range of professions in the UK, including the solicitors' profession and the Bar. An Act of Parliament, the Sex Disqualification (Removal) Act 1919, changed all of this by opening up the professions to women and enabling their appointment to public positions, including on the judiciary. While there was an instant change caused by this Act, including Ada Summers being sworn in as the first woman magistrate on 31 December 1919, widespread progress occurred gradually. The first woman solicitor came in 1920, first barrister in 1922, and first county court judge in 1962.

In 2017, a woman reached the very top of the legal profession when Lady Hale was sworn in as President of the Supreme Court of the United Kingdom. Today, women make up more than half of university law students and trainee solicitors. However, despite Lady Hale's historic achievement, the top levels of the profession are still mostly male and white. Change is happening, but slowly.

Millicent Grant QC (Hon.) CILEx, former President of CILEx

It's wonderful to see the diversity of women who have qualified as lawyers in the UK over the past 100 years, in particular during the years since I entered the profession. Reflecting all streams of the profession – barristers, solicitors and CILEx lawyers – women have taken up roles in industry, started their own legal practices and are holding senior positions in the judiciary. Representing all races and social backgrounds, we continue to break barriers, set trends and become role models for young women of the future.

Sophie-Anna McClintock
Belfast

The past few months have been a difficult time for lawyers
worldwide, with court closures and job uncertainty due to
the COVID-19 pandemic. I will be qualifying as a solicitor in
the coming weeks and starting my career in Phoenix Law
Human Rights Lawyers as a criminal defence solicitor. I hope
in the next 100 years total equality will be visible across the
legal profession.

Amina Brooks
Birmingham

The pandemic and lockdown have made me reflect deeply on my dual role as a mother and a lawyer. I have now decided to start my own small law practice as a self-employed lawyer so I can spend more time with my family.

I also owe my decision to Dana Denis-Smith's quote about her support for women in business.

I hope to use my knowledge of the law to help people in my new venture. This was, after all, the reason I qualified to be a lawyer.

Sophie Kernthaler
Birmingham

I have been fortunate in my career to have been able to work from home for many years, however never to the extent that has been required by the COVID-19 pandemic. I am optimistic that now so many employers have seen that working from home can and does work, more people will be given the flexibility to work differently and in a way that suits their individual circumstances. A move away from rigid office structures and presenteeism can only benefit the diversity of the profession.

Marissa Jacquet
Birmingham

My journey to qualification wasn't easy: my first legal job was on reception and I slowly worked my way up, moving through various firms before securing my training contract and eventually qualifying. Being a woman in law can be challenging: there have been past instances where in meetings with a Partner it has been assumed that I am the PA! At present, I work in a smaller firm. I'm fortunate that the ethos is 'promote from within', and they have been very vocal about encouraging my progression to partnership over time. I know other females in bigger firms struggling to be promoted at the same rate as their male counterparts, and it is disappointing still to see that today.

Over the last few months I've found that my mindset has shifted in respect of my priorities. As a young female lawyer, I have often worried about starting a family and how the timing of that will affect my career, balancing raising a family with the demanding nature of the profession. My hopes are that firms will see the benefit of adopting flexible working styles that mean women don't have to see having a family and a career as a trade-off.

Karen Bailey
Birmingham

There have been many changes since I started practising in the 80s.
There are now far more women in the profession, and I do not
have to try as hard to be taken seriously, which may have been due
to my age, race and gender when I was starting out. While there are
many larger firms, the opportunities for young people to progress to
partnership appear to be shrinking.

The global pandemic has led to stress and uncertainty. Those
who have additional responsibilities while working from home,
such as children or others to care for are sheroes (and heroes,
but the weight of change has fallen mainly on women). I miss the
camaraderie of having everyone together in the office or meeting
people at court. Access to justice is even more of an issue now,
as is ensuring that clients are not disadvantaged by the current
working practices.

However, there has been something heart-warming about peering
into colleagues' rooms at home during remote meetings, catching
glimpses of their other lives and knowing that they are (mostly)
loved and cared for. We have become more considerate of one
another and more open about sharing our concerns and fears.

Olivia Sinclair

Birmingham

I am very lucky to work for a firm which promotes diversity and has recently been listed as the firm with the most female partners in the UK. I have been encouraged and supported by my team throughout lockdown and have found out how adaptable I can be. I have discovered that I am self-motivated and able to use my own initiative whilst I am unable to walk over to a colleague's desk to ask a question. My hope for the future of the legal profession is that we learn from our recent experiences of the COVID-19 and BAME movements and that we continue to encourage diversity and flexibility in the workplace. In turn, I believe that this will pave the way for greater inclusivity.

Madhu Rai
Birmingham

Early in my professional legal career I worked long, hard hours in a predominately male environment, but with perseverance I broke gender and ethnic barriers, and was appointed Chief Crown Prosecutor in 2005. By embracing challenges, from 2008 I led from the front prosecuting serious, complex and sensitive cases at the Crown Court.

Before the COVID-19 pandemic wigs, gowns, jury trials and hearings were the norm in my environment. With the COVID-19 crisis that norm was dramatically revolutionised overnight. The transformation, the new, agile way of working, enabled me and my colleagues to innovate, use new technology via Skype, Microsoft Teams and Common Video Platform to conduct remote court hearings, and changed our culture to balance work and life.

We are increasingly working in a virtual world and I am part of that pioneering change. The future, I believe, is a balance between remote working using technologies and contact in person in other work areas. I envisage lay jurors will remain part of the justice system (although their numbers may reduce) to safeguard the integrity of trials. Discerning facts and the credibility of witnesses is an essential role of jurors who bring with them experience of life.

Virtual working is the future, but we must safeguard against rigid application of artificial intelligence, and cybercrime.

Sarah Newport
Cardiff and Barry

It is not lost on me that I have been able to progress my career without facing instant barriers. This is entirely as a result of the courage and determination of the women who have fought for equality in the profession. These women inspire me every day. We owe it to them to continue their work.

That said, I have faced exclusion from situations where male counterparts have all been invited.

I no longer decide not to complain as others before me have faced much worse – it is my responsibility to call this behaviour out to continue to strive for true equality.

From my observations of the brilliant women who balance their careers and motherhood, I have seen forced flexibility in working practices. I only hope that this continues and will be one of the few positive outcomes of the pandemic.

My hope is for continued diversification on all fronts. Lawyers who overcome challenges, or who take the brave step to join the profession later in life, must see the profession as accessible. I am lucky to know lawyers whose life experience translates into incredible passion for justice.

I hope the legal aid system will, one day, be approached by policymakers with the respect and value it deserves. Legal aid enables some of the most important cases which bring about landmark positive change.

Genevieve Parke
Edinburgh

I recognise that lockdown has damaged workplace equality overall, but my own professional experience has been positive. My husband, who ordinarily works full-time in an inflexible industry, was furloughed whilst I continued to work full-time. Naturally he took over daytime care of our children and I relished not having to juggle childcare arrangements and drop-offs with work.

I work as parliamentary counsel for the Scottish Government, and we had an incredibly busy period working on emergency legislation. I found the long hours so much easier from home and without also having to be the primary caregiver to our children. It was a very rewarding experience that I was glad to be able to commit to single-mindedly.

The experience has revealed that our family is happier if my husband works less and is more involved in domestic life and we are fortunate to be able to make that permanent. Hopefully others will also experience a recalibration of domestic duties. Separately I understand that the private legal sector has seen a newfound willingness to embrace home working, and I hope that this more widespread flexibility will be of lasting benefit to women in law generally.

Madeleine MacKenzie
Edinburgh

Shortly before moving from Inverness to London in 1990 to take up the post of Assistant Scottish Parliamentary Draftsman in the Lord Advocate's Department, I received a letter from the department. Now that it was known that the new recruit was female, the job title had been changed to 'Assistant Scottish Parliamentary Counsel'.

On 30 April 1990 I met my new colleagues. All eight were men. I discovered that only two female lawyers had previously worked in the department. Margaret Christie was the first-ever woman to do so. She was followed by Jennifer Fletcher, who was the first female solicitor to do so (Margaret having been an Advocate).

With the establishment of the Scottish Parliament in 1999, I moved to Edinburgh as one of six founding members of the Scottish Government's Parliamentary Counsel Office. Today thirteen of the twenty-five parliamentary counsel in Edinburgh are female (including Genevieve Parke, who is also in this book).

Two of the four UK drafting offices are currently led by women lawyers for the first time: Elizabeth Gardiner in London and Brenda King in Belfast.

These changes are reflected worldwide, with female parliamentary counsel accounting for a significant proportion of the membership of the Commonwealth Association of Legislative Counsel.

Jenny Broatch
Edinburgh

My experience as a woman in the law has been a positive one. I had a wonderful experience at Edinburgh University being tutored by people like Professor Alexander McCall Smith, for example. I still maintain very close friendships with my friends from the Law degree.

I specialise in family law, an area which is constantly evolving and always interesting. I presently work at Thorntons Law where there is a culture of flexibility and support generally.

I am lucky to have the support of my husband and also my parents and my in-laws who have been extremely helpful in looking after my two sons when that has been needed.

Now we find ourselves in uncharted waters, and everyone is feeling the challenge of combining their working life with their personal commitments. Good employers understand the need to be flexible, realistic and supportive at these difficult times, which will in turn inspire loyalty and commitment from staff.

We need a continuation of the inclusive and progressive thinking that the Law Society of Scotland and a lot of employers are modelling now. Hopefully, some good can come out of this, whether it is flexible working being normalised or the ability to come together in a crisis.

Anita Margaret McNair
Edinburgh

When the pandemic began I briefly worked from home then was placed on furlough. Thankfully I have an amazing employer in the Law Society of Scotland which has continued to make me feel valued and included. My colleagues have been supportive and kept in constant communication. The lockdown has been a time for reflection and introspection and, whilst I have absolutely loved my time at home with family, I am very keen to get back into a workplace that values its colleagues and does its utmost to support women (and men) in law.

Kirsten Leckie
Edinburgh

Generally, I have had a positive experience working in law. However, as a woman in law, I have previously encountered barriers and outdated opinions. I feel that the profession is trying to move towards equality but that we are not there yet. I am hopeful that by the end of my career we (as a society and a profession) will have made even more progress, that the ever-increasing numbers of women entering law translates to more women at the top of the legal profession. I hope that in the future, women in law will walk into a room to see a diverse and equal representation without any pressure to conform to stereotypes.

Over recent months, everyone has adapted to a new way of working, in particular working parents. Employers should recognise the positivity of flexible working for all parents, not just mothers. I hope that all parents are encouraged to work in a way that supports their family life. The profession should embrace these changes in the long term and move away from the 'traditional' views of working practices.

Lindsay Ogunyemi
Glasgow

The pandemic hit us all like a freight train. An unexpected arrival.
Sudden, uninvited. We felt fear, uncertainty, disbelief. Lives and
livelihoods were lost in a matter of weeks.

For me, like most, the changes were immediate. My dining room
became my office. My children, my pupils. My time, double booked.

Adrenalin got me through the first few weeks. After that it was the
warmth and support of my friends, family and colleagues who lifted
me up. Shared experiences. A little chat, a little lift.

I am not sure what the legal world will look like when the dust
settles. Remote working appears to be here to stay. For some it is
a blessing, for others it brings challenges. My hope as a woman
in law is that the pandemic will lead to a more flexible way of
working. A recognition that time spent in the office does not reflect
productivity. Women are resilient and adaptable. These qualities are
required now more than ever.

The pandemic has reminded us how fragile life is and how
important it is to support and lift those around us. If the pandemic
has taught us one thing it is that we are better together.

Safeena Rashid
Glasgow

When I reflect on my experiences within the law over the years, a mix of emotions and feelings surface – happiness, sadness, pride, uncertainty, isolation, camaraderie, stress and excitement among others. This variety is indicative of an evolving career constantly adapting to changing circumstances. Two of the most constant feelings I have as a woman in the law are the sense of awe I feel being in the company of so many trailblazing women and the sense of honour I feel playing a small part in Scotland's legal history, hopefully paving the way for a more female-friendly tomorrow, where the legal profession's sexism and patriarchy are relegated to history. The pandemic having brought trials to a near halt, perhaps the biggest change in my life has been an abundance of time. No longer am I flying from one event to another, but I have time to reflect properly on life. I have used the time to write more, teach more, see my family more and binge-watch Korean dramas more! Reflection gives me optimism about future opportunities that I can carve out as a female lawyer. There will be many – we just need to have the confidence to go for them.

Emma Flood

Glasgow

I am not only a woman in law, but a woman in law and technology. I help bring legal-sector digital projects to life. Until recently, convincing lawyers, law firms and legal organisations that being creative around the use of technology can improve our working lives has been a challenge. As a sector, we are often resistant to change, even where it could benefit us, particularly women, in the long term.

I have been working as part of a team encouraging lawyers in Scotland to come together as a community, access CPD online, and build a hub for legal-sector news and events. As a result of the pandemic, online learning and interaction have become ever more important. Women can be at the forefront of online learning and events, as they are not held back by the traditional barriers of travel and family commitments.

My hope is that we will continue to utilise technology as far as possible. We have the capacity to be a truly innovative sector, not only in terms of how we carry out our work but also in how we manage our work/life balance. Law is so perfectly suited to remote working, flexible work patterns and to leading the way in equality, and the coronavirus pandemic has shown us what is possible.

Eleanor Fry
Leeds

Being a woman in the law is all about time management, and what better way to prove that point than to experience lockdown with two very active toddlers and continuing professional obligations? With newly imposed deadlines requiring a thorough review of ongoing cases, there was reading to be done, video-link conferences to be held and remote meetings and hearings to be conducted, timetabled to accommodate the children's needs and, where possible, my husband's work commitments. I lost count of how many times I heard (senior, male) judges comment upon how much spare time everyone must have these days, as I endeavoured to cancel out the noise of my children shouting for 'Mummy' at the stairgate, while my husband tried to distract them. With the prospect of court sitting hours extending into evenings and weekends, after which preparation is still required to be done (and done properly), it now looks like the real benefit of lockdown, which was spending time together as a family, will be but a distant memory. I live in hope of a better-funded system and a swift return to regular trial listings, perhaps also with some work-free weekends and a solid eight hours' sleep…

Danielle Gilmour
Leeds

My experience as a woman in the law has been non-traditional and occasionally difficult (raised on a council estate, the daughter of a single mum, attending state school) but ultimately is so far successful and, thankfully, no longer unique.

My first professional experiences were positive; I was clerk to a very supportive, fair-minded and encouraging male High Court judge and then I had an able, strong, female pupil supervisor. I have great support and leaders, both male and female, in chambers and I've had excellent work opportunities.

I credit that to two things: my mother who raised me to recognise that I was as worthy and able as anyone who worked hard, and all the women who came before me.

The last few months, however, have shown me that the experience of women is still less visible in the justice system. I'm particularly concerned about plans for extended operating hours and the impact that will have on the many talented female barristers who are also primary carers and who may be forced to sacrifice one of their important roles.

So despite practising at a more diverse and inclusive Bar than the women of the First 100 Years, it seems that the women's work is not yet done and my sincere hope for the future is that one day we finish the job.

Nadya Makarova
Liverpool

I followed the common path of starting a family soon after qualifying and working part-time. This led to having to accept lower positions and pay, and missing out on promotions. I was once told that, if I was full-time, my pay would be higher. Now we do not have to be in the office 9–5, we can work flexible hours and from home. The impact will be huge for women who are primary carers for their children, because there is no pressure to stay late at work and miss out on family time or sacrifice your career in favour of being a mum.

I was able to do 9am PE with Joe and homeschool. In June, I was able to walk my daughter to school without rushing her to make my train, and pick her up instead of her having to attend an after-school club. Some days I have family time between 3.30–7pm and work after. I am confident that I will be better at work/life balance by working 2–3 days a week from home: I will keep up with walking to school and be there to collect at least a couple of times a week. I wish this had been possible when my children were smaller.

Susanna McGibbon
London

I have been privileged to coordinate the legal support to government in response to the crisis. Colleagues across departments have dealt with novel and urgent legal issues with commitment and dedication. From primary legislation completed at record speed to Regulations produced overnight (again and again); innovative commercial deals to advice on safe workplaces; draconian restrictions on behaviour to economic interventions supporting business and those unable to work. I have been proud to witness the collaboration, mutual support and empathetic leadership amongst the lawyers working to tackle the virus's impact on us all. Many of those colleagues have been juggling childcare and home schooling whilst meeting impossible deadlines and challenging client demands. The Government Legal Department (GLD) has championed flexible working for many years, but we have seen that more widespread remote working has been a great leveller – in legal delivery, in leadership and in the connectedness of our teams across the country. Whilst we all look forward to some rebalancing, my hope is that across the legal profession we take this opportunity to re-imagine our workplaces as valuable collaboration and teamwork spaces; to build rewarding careers that aren't dependent on being in London; and to lead with the compassion and open-mindedness that has been so crucial to our success.

Anna Sanders

London

The Government Legal Department (GLD) has risen to dealing with the challenge of COVID-19 with the professionalism and expertise that government lawyers are known for. I am proud to be a member of the GLD Executive Team and Board supporting all our people to fulfil our core purpose: to help the government to govern well, within the rule of law – something that has not changed in the current environment. I hope that we continue to increase our diversity as an organisation, reflecting the society we represent and serve.

Therese G. Prince
London

2019 saw us celebrating the centenary of women in the law. It was an exciting time to be a woman lawyer. A time to reflect on how far we've come and to embrace the possibilities of tomorrow. As we embarked on 2020, I felt ready for what the future held and the role I would play. Then suddenly our world changed.

For many the last few months have been challenging to say the least! That has been no different for me as I have navigated the merging of home and professional life, postponed events and sought to stay afloat in our ever-changing world. In the midst of a global pandemic which has wreaked havoc on our societal institutions we have seen issues of racial inequity and injustice rise to the surface, bringing with it more challenges to tackle. This has made me more passionate about the law. My hope is for a profession that fulfils its duty to uphold the rule of law, defend the vulnerable, speak for the voiceless and lead by example. I recently heard that every challenge is an opportunity – I can't wait to see what we do with the opportunity that has been presented to us.

Helen Jennings
London

Since this photo was taken I moved home to Ireland over the months of COVID-19-related lockdown, completed most of my Bar Professional Training Course (BPTC) exams and secured pupillage. Like everyone else, I also witnessed a new surge in action on the issue of racial inequality globally. The Black Lives Matter movement became the most urgent call for civil and equal rights I have seen within my lifetime in the UK and Ireland. As a human rights activist and aspiring barrister, I have deeply reflected on the part I will play in this movement. I have become more aware of the ways in which my actions are complicit in upholding racist power structures. This includes my role within the justice system. I am working to educate myself and identify ways in which I can be actively anti-racist in my personal life, my campaigning and my career.

The Repeal jumper I'm wearing in this picture is an emblem of the struggle for reproductive rights in Ireland. As an activist in that struggle, I experienced the enormous power of grassroots organising. Now the jumper stands to remind me of the importance of solidarity between oppressed social groups. The Repeal campaign brought together all sections of Irish society, all demographics, at home and in the diaspora. As women, as women in the law, much progress has been made towards our equal rights over the past 100 years. It is time to use our positions of privilege to stand with other groups, demanding equality for all. My hope for the future of the profession is for greater equality in access to legal careers, for all who share a passion for the law and for justice regardless of the circumstances of their birth or identity. A further hope is that the legal profession will strongly support the demands of people of colour, LGBT+ people, and other oppressed groups for their full and equal rights, fair treatment and freedom from discrimination. Here's hoping for the next 100 years – to a brighter future.

Alison Eddy
London

The way I've worked as a lawyer for over thirty years has changed from working excessive hours in an office to working digitally at home. Pre-pandemic, 43% of our colleagues were working flexibly, while now over 80% have told us ideally they want a blend of working from home and in the office. The pandemic has accelerated a welcome change in attitude towards flexible working, often seen as a barrier to women moving into senior roles.

The pandemic has created a window into colleagues' lives. We have all had time to reflect and reprioritise. Some colleagues, particularly those juggling childcare, have found working from home a challenge, and I've become very aware of the need to check in, help build resilience and focus on their wellbeing.

The future is bright for young lawyers. We have more senior female role models, 43% of our partners, helping to create a belief that it's possible to reach the top and sharing their stories. We now need to address not just gender but intersectionality, putting an action plan in place. We know what matters is what gets measured. Reporting on gender and now ethnicity pay gaps has been a positive step forward, helping to address inequalities.

Glenda Vencatachellum
London

It's been challenging but rewarding.

Since the start of my career, many preconceptions regarding women in the law have changed.

I stayed the course. I was a member of chambers for many years. I have now set up on my own. Many of my female contemporaries left the independent Bar, seeking security. As regards work/life balance, advances in technology are a mixed blessing. The time saved travelling to pick up briefs is now spent organising emailed briefs and taking out-of-hours calls.

I reflect that women in England were first called to the Bar shortly after the last pandemic. During the current pandemic, the Family Court has conducted hearings by telephone. The focus has remained on the quality of advocacy. Preconceptions or unconscious bias from visual cues have lessened. Simultaneously taking instructions via other media, whilst conducting a telephone hearing, has been challenging; we rise to the challenge.

I hope that in the future there is more cross-over between previously gender-stereotyped areas of legal practice. I hope to make progress in international commercial arbitration.

Every day in practice, despite the many professional and personal pressures, I feel privileged to be able to take my part in the process of the justice system.

Chiamaka Ruth Ike
London

I was excited to be a part of the 'Face the Future' campaign because of the message it delivers. I got stuck in with the logistics and offered my capacity to assist the photographer on the day (a bonus was me getting my pictures taken first to test out the settings, and learning a few tricks!). My experience as a woman in the law has been pleasant and this, I would argue, is mostly attributable to the fact that I am in the civil service. Whilst there is still a lot of progress and movement needed, I believe the civil service is committed to addressing and closing any gender gap and discrepancies. I find that there is a lot of flexibility and opportunity for development and some encouragement of diversity, at least in my department and my experience. I am currently in the process of qualifying as a Chartered Legal Executive Lawyer through the Home Office. Living through a global pandemic has made me appreciate my role as a woman in the law, because I have not experienced major changes to my work and I was easily able to adapt to the current climate because I had a flexible working arrangement – for example, I used to work from home several days a week prior to the pandemic, so it was a smooth transition. My hope for the future is to see more women of ethnic background in senior roles as Grade 5 lawyers, barristers and also more female judges as the norm. It is my desire to set an example and inspire the younger generation of BAME community women to pursue a career in law. I hope to leave a legacy!

Cris McCurley
Newcastle

As a specialist working with women and children who have been abused, lockdown has been a period when we have seen a surge in demand for legal protection and also intense work towards change, both in terms of the Domestic Abuse Bill scrutiny and amendments, and the report of the MOJ expert inquiry into how well the family courts manage private cases involving children when the issue of vulnerability and abuse is raised. It has been a high-octane but exciting period of time in terms of both client work and input into the Bill and inquiry. I am so proud of all of us who contributed to the inquiry report and the Bill, and while I'm devastated that the vote in Parliament went against DA protection for all migrant women as opposed to just those on a spouse visa (and there is more work to be done on this issue to achieve equality), I feel rejuvenated going forward, confident that we will see a far better, safer response for the victims of abuse and their children. I see a hopeful future, and it's very exciting!

Karen H. Kabweru-Namulemu
Nottingham

As a black woman, my journey to the Bar has not been easy. The word 'perseverance' immediately comes to mind. I have faced knockbacks and had to gain experience beyond academia to get here.

I am proud to work in a rewarding profession. I smile when I see my red bag for work on a complex case or think of my positions in chambers and on circuit. They are reminders of what I can achieve.

Lockdown has changed how I work and interact. It has brought isolation; remote working; technological advances (and issues!); forced changes to advocacy and client care; and removed an element of the human touch.

However, for me, lockdown will be characterised by the killing of George Floyd and the world's response. This brought into sharp focus my experiences and those of others and put the spotlight on challenges and inequalities for black and minority individuals at the Bar and within society. My hope is that the momentum and desire for change continues and I see a more diverse and representative profession; from those that sit on the Bench to our wonderful court staff. I am the Bar and I will be a part of that change.

Christine Doughty
Nottingham

When the photographs were taken we had no idea that, within
a couple of weeks, the world as we knew it would have changed
and is unlikely to go back to what it was. In Nottingham we were
looking forward to the Law Society AGM, the annual Awards Dinner,
and a twinning visit to Germany. They all fell down like a pack
of cards, together with the rest of our professional and personal
commitments. We could no longer be suspicious of video calls and
conference meetings and before we knew it we were Zooming the
day away. This would have been unheard of in my early days when
the electric typewriter was a novelty, and a photocopier was a messy
invention which required some skill. All office calls went through the
switchboard operator and emails and mobile phones were not on
the horizon. Working mothers, amongst others, may welcome a 'new
normal' where the majority of work is done from home and training
is done online. I would offer a word of caution and look back on the
influences on my career. Learning the law takes a lifetime, and much
knowledge is gained from our elders and our peers. Interaction
at courses and conferences has as much value as the lectures, and
the contacts we make can never be replaced by a face on a screen.
It is worth considering how long we may spend worrying about a
problem in splendid isolation when five minutes queuing with a
colleague for the coffee machine could solve it.

Lana Antoniv
Nottingham

My photo was taken in the days before the global pandemic began to impact on so many of us and I could still easily travel to the Law Society office to take this photo.

As a woman in law, my route to qualifying as a solicitor was a long one, delayed by taking care of my family, working and studying part-time to enable qualification.

It hasn't changed much for me in the last few months. All the things I became used to and perfected, whilst juggling work, study and family, such as organising, planning ahead and multi-tasking, worked well for me during lockdown. With limited accommodation space, with both myself and my partner working from home and taking care of our son, James, we worked split shifts to look after him. We fitted our work desk in our bedroom (due to lack of other space), bought additional IT equipment and planned well. It took some adapting in the first few weeks of lockdown, but soon it worked like a well-oiled machine. I established our routine early and this helped us to adapt quickly, without any major issues. Being a mother helped me tremendously during this time – the multi-tasking, the organising and the planning came in all too useful and the lockdown didn't affect us much because of it.

I was fortunate my employer allowed me flexible working time, as this allowed for the split shift at home. I hope any future employer is as flexible and takes into account childcare provision. I hope that 9–5 hours will no longer be the norm, but instead the hours individuals decide to work, which suit them and their family.

Naomi De Silva
Nottingham

As a female and as an ethnic minority, my journey in law has not been straightforward. I often made myself smaller and adopted roles that would help me to integrate.

I was on maternity leave when this photo was taken. I had learned that I had imposter syndrome. Law both controls and exacerbates the feelings of inadequacy and anxiety.

The photoshoot helped remind me that I had worked hard for my career. Now I am working hard to be a good mother. Lockdown provided an opportunity for intimate family time. I hope that the changes to working practices do not stop women's progress.

There is still a long way to go for women to be equal in law and even further for ethnic minorities. I am grateful to the women who paved the way before me and for parents who made me believe that I was equal to all. I am lucky to have had strong female role models in my mother and grandmothers. I love my partner for never doubting my ability. If one person looks at my photo and thinks, 'If she can do it then so can I,' that would be a wonderful thing.

Alice Devenuto
Oxford

As a woman pursuing a BA in Law, I have been exposed to the underwhelming representation of women in the field, in both academic and professional realms. Luckily, my experience at the University of Oxford has been positively affected by the increasing number of women who, like me, have embarked on the study of the Law, and who work to create networks to support each other.

The outbreak of coronavirus marked a forced break away from such positive relations. Not being able to interact as easily with other women facing the same challenges as myself, and not being able to turn to them for inspiration and comfort, has proven difficult, especially as I was sitting my final exams.

In 2021, I will begin my journey as a trainee solicitor in London. I hope that the progress made during the past few months with the use of online platforms will result in a more widespread adoption of flexible working. I think this would facilitate greater representation of women in the profession, especially at more senior levels. I aspire to reach these without compromising on having an equally fulfilling personal life.

Laura Hoyano
Oxford and London

I have enjoyed fulfilling dual careers in the law, as a barrister practising first in Canada and then in England, and as an academic at the University of Oxford Faculty of Law and Wadham College, Oxford. My legal careers have spanned forty years and seen many battles for women's equality in the professions (I was the only woman partner in my Canadian law firm's head office, when maternity leave was a bizarre notion). As an academic I've focused on nurturing the lawyers of the future, especially women, to give them the courage to forge their own pathways. The English court system came to an abrupt halt with lockdown, and the criminal justice system is flat on the floor. I'm dismayed that I may never again be in a courtroom. Women barristers have been particularly hard-hit. We cannot allow the pandemic to sap our determination to continue the drive for diversity in the legal professions. I've faith in the resilience and determination of the extraordinary lawyers whom I've taught, and those with whom I work. I'm inspired by those supporting the Black Lives Matter movement globally. They continue their predecessors' work to effect the fundamental changes essential to a just society.

This edition © Scala Arts & Heritage
Publishers Ltd, 2021
Text and images © Next 100 Years, 2021

First published in 2021 by
Scala Arts & Heritage Publishers Ltd
27 Old Gloucester Street
London WC1N 3AX, United Kingdom
www.scalapublishers.com

In association with Next 100 Years
www.first100years.org.uk

ISBN 978-1-78551-361-9

Designed by James Alexander
at Jade Design/www.jadedesign.co.uk
Editing and translation by Neil Titman
Printed and bound in Turkey

10 9 8 7 6 5 4 3 2 1

**Photographers for the 'Face the Future'
sessions:**
Zahara Abdul, María José Alós, Thomas
Appert, Maja Baska, Marcus Bevis, Dave
Chakrabarti, Chris de Beer, Jay Glenn, Simon
Graham, Marcus Jamieson-Pond, Richard
Jones, Paul Lyme, Alix McIntosh, Neil Miller,
Daniel Novotny, Jess Pearson, Didier Plowy,
Marlene Rahmann, Sam Toolsie, Tammy Van
Nerum, Juliana Vasquez, Jamie Williamson,
Alex Wroblewski, Jazpar Yeo.

Acknowledgements
We would like to thank Marcus Jamieson-
Pond for his excellent work as Creative
Director of the 'Face the Future' photography
day and for his help in selecting photos
for inclusion in this book. We are grateful
to our wonderful hosts of the 'Face the
Future' photography sessions around the
world. Your help was key in bringing the
campaign to life and making it such a
success. We would also like to thank
Angela Holdsworth for graciously offering
her feedback on the book.